Cross-Stitch a
Beautiful Christmas

Cross-Stitch a Beautiful Christmas

Jutta Lammèr

 Sterling Publishing Co., Inc.   New York

Translated by Elisabeth E. Reinersmann
Drawings by Ekkehard Dreschel
Photographs by Thomas A. Weiss
Edited by Barbara Busch

Library of Congress Cataloging-in-Publication Data

Lammèr, Jutta.
   [Sticken für Weihnachten. English]
   Cross-stitch a beautiful Christmas / by Jutta Lammèr ;
[photography, Thomas Weiss ; drawings, Ekkehard Drechsel].
      p.   cm.
   Translation of: Sticken für Weihnachten.
   Includes index.
   ISBN 0-8069-8310-8
   1. Cross-stitch—Patterns.   2. Christmas decorations. I. Title.
TT778.C76L3713   1990   91-12851
746.44'3041—dc20   CIP

[CIP]

10 9 8 7 6 5 4 3 2 1

First paperback edition published in 1992 by
Sterling Publishing Company, Inc.
387 Park Avenue South, New York, N.Y. 10016
English translation © 1991 by Sterling Publishing Company
Original edition published under the title
Sticken für Weihnachten © 1990 by
Ravensburger Buchverlag Otto Maier GmbH
Distributed in Canada by Sterling Publishing
% Canadian Manda Group, P.O. Box 920, Station U
Toronto, Ontario, Canada M8Z 5P9
Distributed in Great Britain and Europe by Cassell PLC
Villiers House, 41/47 Strand, London WC2N 5JE
Distributed in Australia by Capricorn Link Ltd.
P.O. Box 665, Lane Cove, NSW 2066

Printed in Hong Kong
All rights reserved

Sterling   ISBN 0-8069-8310-8   Trade
                 0-8069-8311-6   Paper

INTRODUCTION

Although it requires concentration, cross-stitching is one of the most relaxing of all pursuits.

A finished cross-stitching project, however, often looks easier than it actually is, and only those with experience know its degree of difficulty. Beginners, therefore, are well advised not to be too ambitious. For their first project they might want to choose a motif from the sampler on page 59. The border design on pages 20 and 21 can also be used for small, single projects. For those who have just discovered this form of simple needlework, every sampler provided has an estimate of the amount of time needed to finish the project. As with all endeavors, there are those who work rapidly and those who need a bit more time. For some the process itself is the joy, while for others it is the finished project that matters.

The book you hold in your hand presents a wide range of motifs for the Christmas season, including both traditional and modern; some are easy, some more difficult. Each is accompanied by detailed instructions, and whatever your level of expertise there is something to provide you with enjoyment.

TECHNIQUE

Cross-stitching is accomplished by first making an understitch, going from the lower left to the upper right, and then the topstitch, which goes in the opposite direction. It is important that this technique is adhered to for each and every cross-stitch in order to achieve a uniform surface. Always complete one row of understitches in one direction before going on to do the topstitch in the opposite direction. It does not matter if you opt for the up-and-down or the left-to-right method. Just make sure you choose one of the two and stick with it.

Work in horizontal rows, using linen as the base material, carry the embroidery floss from the back to the front between two threads of the material. Then guide the thread diagonally across two "squares." as shown, and carry the embroidery floss from the front to the back of the linen. Continue until the row is finished (see illustration a). Complete the row with the topstitch, working in the opposite direction and using the same holes that were used for the understitch (see illustration b). Care should be taken that each stitch is completed cleanly. This means that while making the stitch, the embroidery needle does not split either the thread of the linen or the embroidery floss already in place. The embroidery floss on the back of your project will run vertically (see the illustration on page 7).

To work the vertical rows, carry the embroidery floss from the back of the material to the front and proceed by guiding it diagonally across two threads of the linen. The floss can then be pulled through to the back of the material and the next step done separately. It is, however, possible to guide the needle horizontally underneath two threads of the linen (see illustration c) which would then become the first step for the next stitch. For the topstitch proceed in the same way, but in the opposite direction (see illustration d on this page). The embroidery thread in the back will run horizontally (see the illustration d on page 7).

Make sure that the embroidery floss lies flat and even on the surface and the linen does not pucker up underneath the stitches. The overall appearance of your project will be more pleasing if the understitch is carried out with a bit more tension than the topstitch.

In order to avoid pulling the floss through to the front when starting a new strand, make a loop at the end of the floss rather than a knot. The loop can easily be undone and the end of the floss hidden under the already existing stitches. Most experienced embroiderers make sure that the end of a new strand is positioned parallel to the row that has just been finished. In this way it will be covered automatically during the process of stitching the next row.

Generations of embroidery enthusiasts have used the traditional horizontal method: starting at the bottom row and, row by row working up to the top row. But lately the vertical method has become popular, working from the left to the right side. When making the topstitch, using the vertical method, the needle for each stitch that pulls floss through the linen from front to back is carried out in a free space (see illustration c), while for the stitch that pulls the floss through the linen from back to front the needle is used in the same hole that was used in the previous row (see diagram d).

It is easier to control a needle when stitching through the linen from front to back. It therefore makes sense to start work on the top, when using the vertical method, and at the bottom, when using the horizontal method. This is particularly important when more than one strand of embroidery floss is used in the same hole. It is much easier to make a precise stitch when the needle is guided from the front to the back. Trying to guide a needle from the back to the front is much more difficult. Another advantage: when going from front to back, the embroidery floss can pull a slightly frayed floss from a neighboring stitch down with it. Going from back to front only increases the fraying.

Photos on the opposite page show the difference between the traditional and the newer method: e and f are done horizontally, g and h vertically.

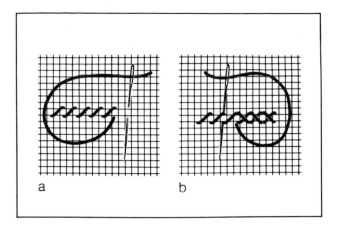

a   b

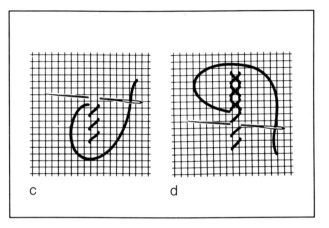

c   d

WORKING WITH PATTERNS AND SYMBOLS

Most of the samples in this book are shown on the right-hand pages, with the patterns and list of symbols on the left-hand pages providing the numbers representing the respective colors used for the project (see display on pages 10/11). In cases where it cannot be shown on the left side, a notation is made of where to find it. Each symbol represents one cross-stitch. One cross-stitch is carried out over a square of two threads of the embroidery linen.

Before starting your project, determine the center of the material as well as the center of the pattern. The center is the intersecting point of the vertical and horizontal midline. An accurate center will assure a properly placed motif on the embroidery linen. Counting and transferring a pattern to the linen is not difficult when the motif is

small. A small ruler or piece of cardboard is all that is needed to stay in the row you are working on.

For larger projects with many different colors the following suggestions will make the job easier: copy the sampler you have chosen and attach the copy to a piece of Styrofoam (you can obtain from a furniture or appliance store.) Use two pins to mark the end and the beginning of the row you intend to work on. If necessary, use a third pin to mark the point at which you intend to interrupt your work. This eliminates any confusion.

(Please note that in some instances the patterns of the samplers are not always on the same page. If such is the case, the necessary information is given).

EMBROIDERY LINEN

Every sampler in this book has been embroidered on #12-linen. This means that since cross- and backstitches are stitched over two threads, a thread count of 12 gives 6×6 cross-stitches. This enables you to determine the size of a finished project. With the exception of border designs for

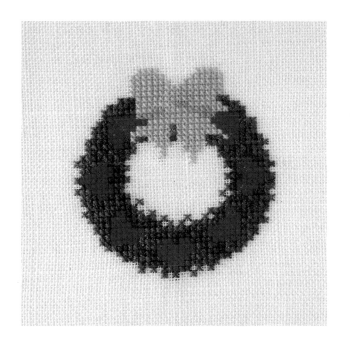

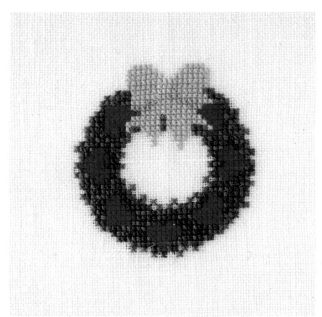

tablecloth and table runners on pages 20/21, we have provided the measurements for each finished project. However, measurements and thread count may differ from one linen to another. If, for instance, #10.5-linen is used, two threads will accommodate 5¼ cross-stitches and the over-all size of the finished project will be larger. The wreaths displayed above show the difference: the wreath on the left was embroidered on linen #10.5; the wreath on the right was embroidered on linen #12.

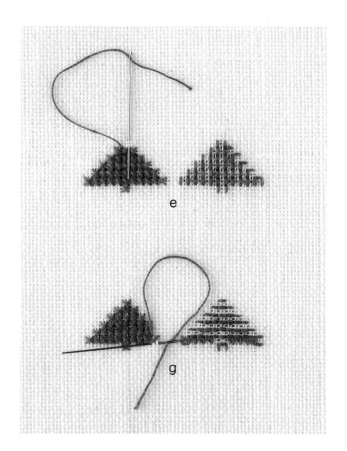

e

g

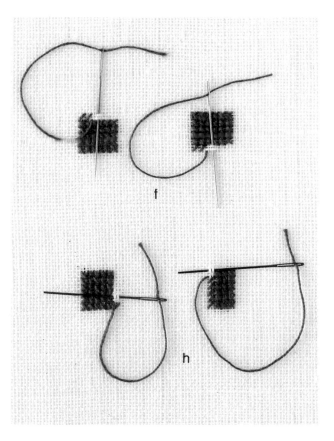

f

h

Besides linen, the classical material used in Denmark, other materials are often chosen. The best known is aida-cloth, made specifically for cross-stitch. Only one thread is used for each cross-stitch with these two materials. Single-strand stramin is also used for cross-stitch projects, and, here too, only one strand is used for each cross-stitch. The photos below show four finished projects each embroidered on different materials: upper left on linen #12; upper right on aida-cloth; lower left on practice cloth; lower right on single-strand stramin. With the exception of the upper left sampler (on linen #12), which measures 3,6 cm in height, all projects are 3,1 cm in height.

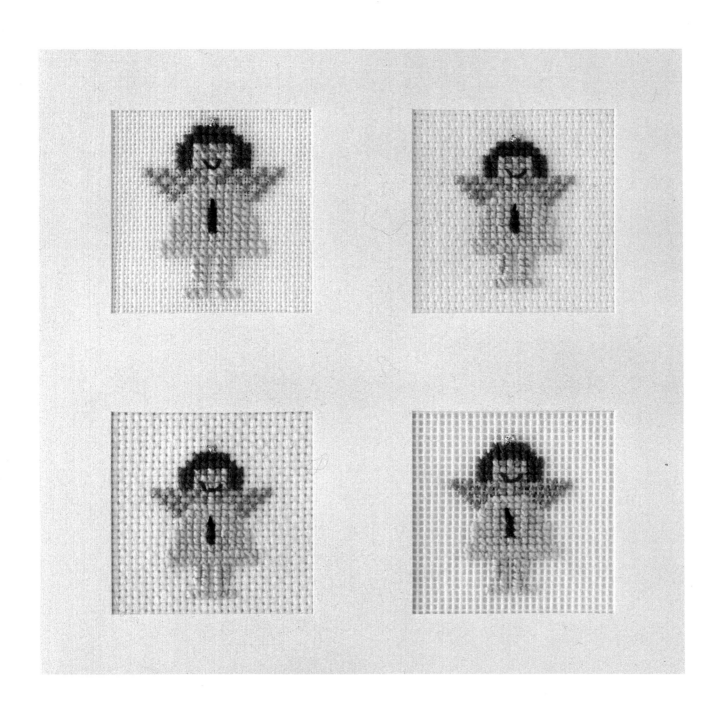

The samplers in this book were all made with MEZ embroidery floss; the charts show the MEZ numbers. For those who prefer DMC or J. & P. Coats embroidery floss, the following numbers are suggested as possible alternatives.

MEZ	DMC	J. & P. COATS	MEZ	DMC	J. & P. COATS	MEZ	DMC	J. & P. COATS	MEZ	DMC	J. & P. COATS	MEZ	DMC	J. & P. COATS
1	Snow white	1	112	550	4107	242	368	6016	351	355	2339	869	211	4303
2	ecru	1002	117	800	7021	243	368	6016	352	801	5475	870	315	3082
6	948	2331	118	813	7161	244	320	6017	355	301	—	871	316	3081
8	754	2331	119	550	4107	245	320	6017	357	918	3340	872	902	3083
9	819	3280	120	828	7053	246	367	6018	358	801	5475	873	902	3083
10	3326	3126	121	3325	7976	253	772	6250	359	300	—	875	3053	6315
11	892	3152	123	312	7979	254	472	6253	360	433	5471	876	320	6017
13	349	2335	127	823	7982	255	472	6253	361	738	5375	877	731	—
19	817	2335	128	828	7053	256	704	6238	362	437	5942	878	701	6226
20	815	3000	129	828	7053	257	3347	6266	363	436	5943	879	502	6876
22	304	3401	130	809	7021	258	3346	6258	365	407	—	880	225	3239
23	963	3280	131	799	7030	259	369	6015	366	677	—	881	738	5375
24	963	3280	132	796	7100	260	369	6015	367	945	3335	882	437	5942
25	776	3281	133	824	7182	261	368	6016	368	729	—	883	922	3336
26	603	3001	134	796	7100	262	367	6018	369	919	2326	884	976	2308
27	604	3001	144	800	7021	263	319	6246	370	434	5000	885	822	—
28	309	3284	145	519	7162	264	369	6015	371	433	5471	886	739	5369
29	600	3056	146	826	7180	265	368	6016	372	738	5375	887	738	5375
35	606	2334	147	825	7181	266	320	6017	373	435	5371	888	437	5942
41	892	3152	148	796	7100	267	989	6266	374	434	5000	889	433	5471
42	498	3410	149	820	7024	268	987	6258	375	436	5943	890	437	5942
43	902	3083	150	820	7024	269	986	6258	376	950	2336	891	783	—
44	814	3044	152	823	7982	278	734	—	378	435	5371	892	353	3006
46	892	3152	158	828	7053	279	734	—	380	938	5477	893	776	3281
47	498	3410	159	827	7159	280	832	—	381	938	5477	894	761	3068
48	3689	3086	160	800	7021	281	830	—	382	898	5476	895	3688	387
49	776	3281	161	793	—	288	744	2293	387	712	5387	896	815	3000
50	963	3280	162	809	7021	289	445	2288	388	3047	2300	897	814	3044
52	3326	3126	164	824	7182	290	726	2294	390	739	5369	900	644	—
54	893	3152	167	3325	7976	291	726	2294	391	372	—	901	436	5943
59	815	3000	168	334	7977	292	745	2296	392	371	—	903	434	5000
65	902	3083	169	798	7022	293	745	2296	393	610	—	905	838	5381
66	962	3151	170	824	7182	295	727	2289	397	762	8510	907	725	2298
68	326	3401	185	747	7053	297	726	2294	398	415	8510	920	809	7021
69	814	3044	186	747	7053	298	725	2298	399	415	8510	921	809	7021
70	814	3044	187	993	6185	300	744	2293	400	414	8513	922	311	7980
72	902	3083	188	993	6185	302	725	2298	401	413	—	925	740	2099
73	819	3280	189	992	6186	303	972	2307	403	310	8403	926	739	5369
74	818	3281	203	369	6015	304	741	2314	410	996	7001	928	828	7053
75	3354	3003	204	369	6015	305	783	—	433	995	7010	929	813	7161
76	603	300L	205	955	6030	306	783	—	778	963	3280	930	518	—
77	309	3284	206	504	6875	308	921	—	830	842	5933	936	434	5000
78	3350	3004	208	503	6879	309	436	5943	831	841	5376	939	809	7021
85	3689	3086	209	3364	6010	310	300	—	832	433	5471	941	825	7181
86	3688	3087	210	562	6213	311	725	2298	843	3012	—	943	782	—
87	3326	3126	211	562	6213	313	402	—	844	471	6010	944	801	5475
88	335	3283	212	3363	6317	314	742	2303	845	732	—	945	734	—
89	601	3128	213	762	6250	316	920	3337	846	938	5477	956	644	—
95	211	4303	214	415	8510	323	742	2303	847	762	8510	972	815	3000
96	210	4303	215	524	6315	324	920	3337	848	415	8510	975	747	7053
97	210	4303	216	523	6316	326	349	2335	849	318	8511	976	747	7053
98	209	4302	217	523	6316	328	351	3011	850	414	8513	977	519	—
99	208	4301	218	3363	6317	329	608	2332	851	823	—	978	793	—
100	550	4107	225	368	6016	330	608	2332	852	739	5369	979	791	7024
101	552	4092	226	368	6016	332	970	2327	853	840	5379	4146	776	3281
102	550	4107	227	320	6017	333	970	2327	854	640	5393	5968	355	2339
104	211	4303	228	367	6018	334	946	2330	856	434	5000	5975	760	3069
105	210	4303	229	987	6258	335	891	3254	858	642	—	8581	318	8511
107	553	4097	230	368	6016	338	970	2327	859	840	5379	9575	3328	3071
108	210	4303	238	907	6001	339	971	2099	860	3346	6258			
109	552	4092	239	906	6256	341	918	3340	861	3346	6258			
110	552	4092	240	369	6015	347	758	2337	862	367	6018			
111	550	4107	241	369	6015	349	434	5000	868	554	4104			

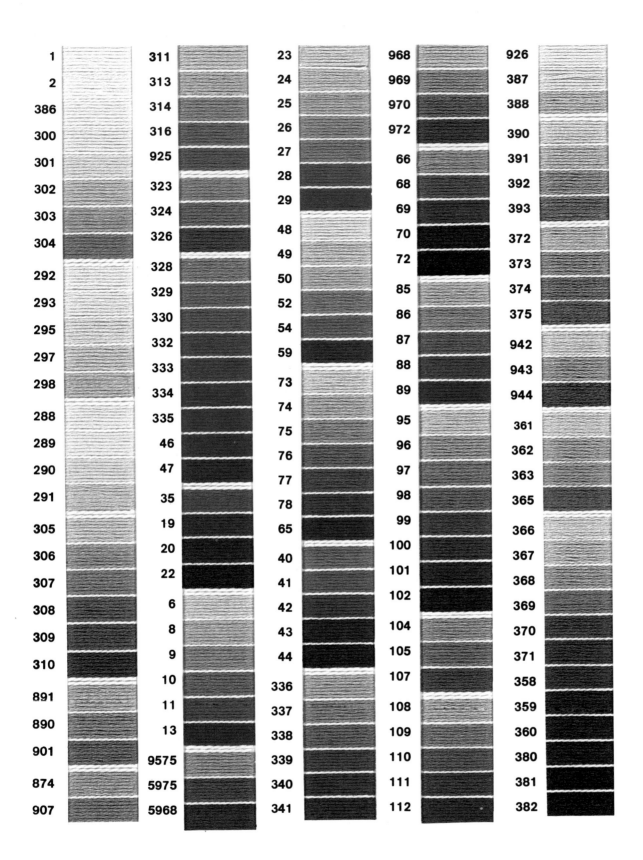

Color chart for MEZ ⚓ embroidery floss

When buying the embroidery floss, please note the following: A zero in front of the color number of the wrapper around the floss means that the strand of floss is 8m (the normal length is 10).

10

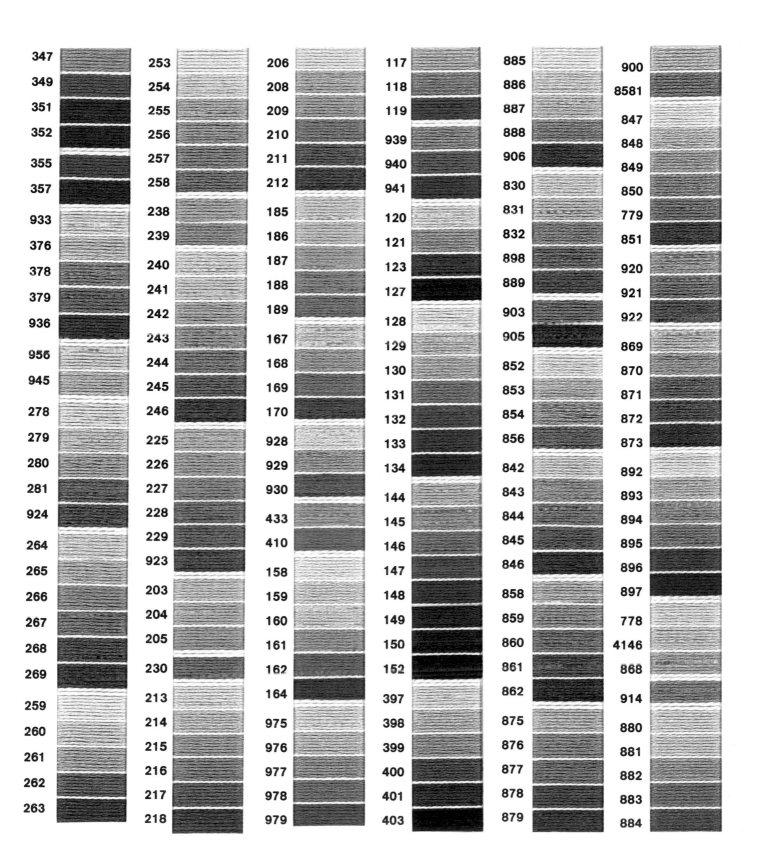

347
349
351
352
355
357
933
376
378
379
936
956
945
278
279
280
281
924
264
265
266
267
268
269
259
260
261
262
263

253
254
255
256
257
258
238
239
240
241
242
243
244
245
246
225
226
227
228
229
923
203
204
205
230
213
214
215
216
217
218

206
208
209
210
211
212
185
186
187
188
189
167
168
169
170
928
929
930
433
410
158
159
160
161
162
164
975
976
977
978
979

117
118
119
939
940
941
120
121
123
127
128
129
130
131
132
133
134
144
145
146
147
148
149
150
152
397
398
399
400
401
403

885
886
887
888
906
830
831
832
898
889
903
905
852
853
854
856
842
843
844
845
846
858
859
860
861
862
875
876
877
878
879

900
8581
847
848
849
850
779
851
920
921
922
869
870
871
872
873
892
893
894
895
896
897
778
4146
868
914
880
881
882
883
884

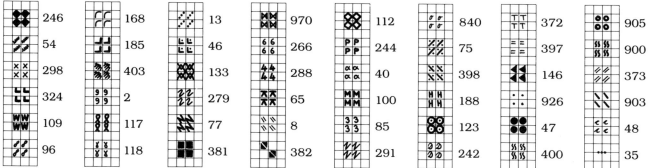

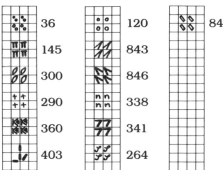	36		120		84
	145		843		
	300		846		
	290		338		
	360		341		
	403		264		

It is best to start this sampler in the middle of one of the packages and continue to work from there up, down, and sideways respectively.

Size of sample: 6¾ × 6 inches (17 × 15cm)

Time required: appr. 20 hours

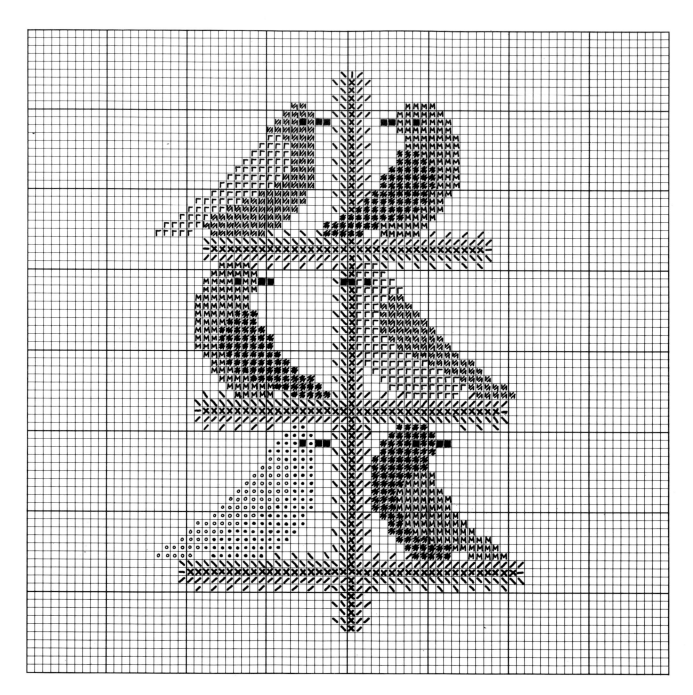

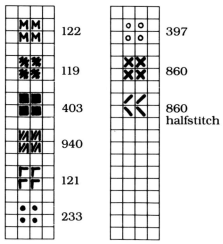

M M / M M	122	
❋ ❋ / ❋ ❋	119	
■ ■ / ■ ■	403	
ⱶ ⱶ / ⱶ ⱶ	940	
Γ Γ / Γ Γ	121	
• • / • •	233	

o o / o o	397	
✕ ✕ / ✕ ✕	860	
╱ ╱ / ╱ ╱	860 halfstitch	

The colors and shapes of these feathered winter friends are reminiscent of Scandinavian embroidery.

The needles of the evergreen branches are half-stitches, alternating between under- and top-stitches.

Size: 4¾ × 3¼ inches (12 × 8cm)

Time: appr. 8 hours

These border motifs are particularly suitable for use in table runners, throws, and place mats. However, they can also be used individually to create greeting cards, napkin holders, or bookmarks.

The needles of the evergreen twigs are half-stitches pointing either left or right.

The pair of birds in the last row can be done as a separate motif (as shown in the left half of the row), or they can be done continuously (as shown in the right half).

The patterns for these motifs are on pages 18 through 21.

(#267: halfstitch; #403: wick; #268: halfstitch)

Symbol	No.
MM MM	121
77 77	313
XX	267
KK	267 halfstitch
▮	403 wick
== ==	301
♡♡ ♡♡	47
OO OO	324
●● ●●	46
NN NN	59
>> >>	398
⊤⊤ ⊤⊤	73
◔◔	146
■■ ■■	403
⠿⠿	268
⠇⠇	268 halfstitch
TT TT	269

Symbol	No.
oo oo	906
SS SS	393
XX XX	298
⋊⋉ ⋊⋉	119
t t t t	48
3 3 3 3	117
HH HH	372
◉◉ ◉◉	145
♥ ♥ ♥ ♥	35
0 0 0 0	397
• • • •	2
ε ε ε ε	49
KK KK	118
ſſ ſſ	358
◆◆	269
4 4 4 4	891
⫽⫽	400

Symbol	No.
∧∧ ∧∧	890
♪♪ ♪♪	360
8 8 8 8	920
WW WW	849
o o o o	847
ᒐᒐ	218

16

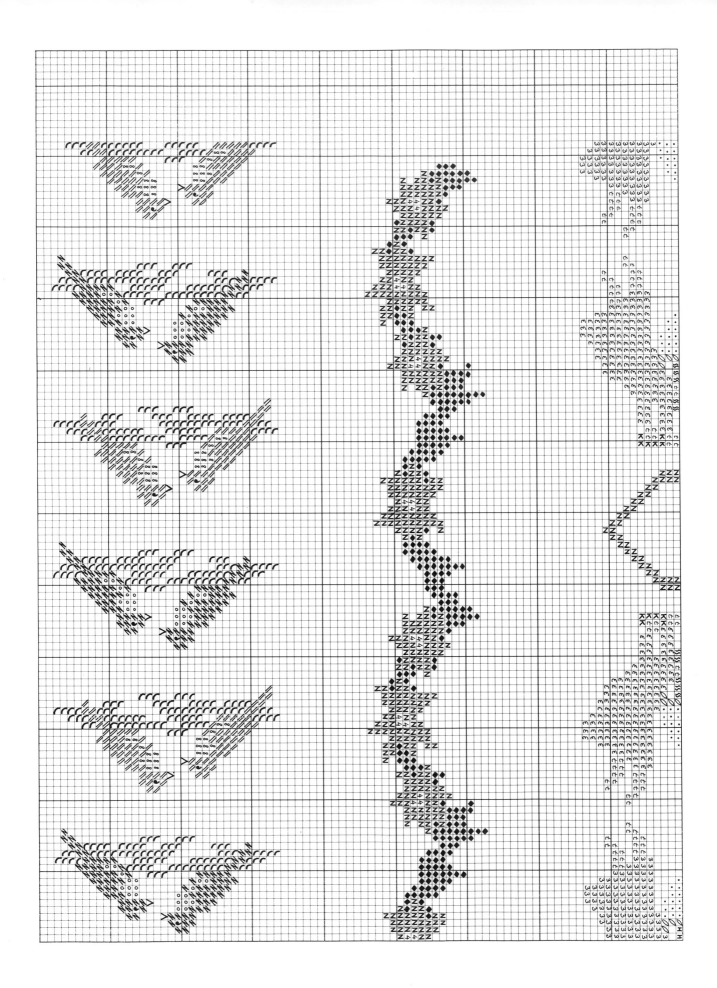

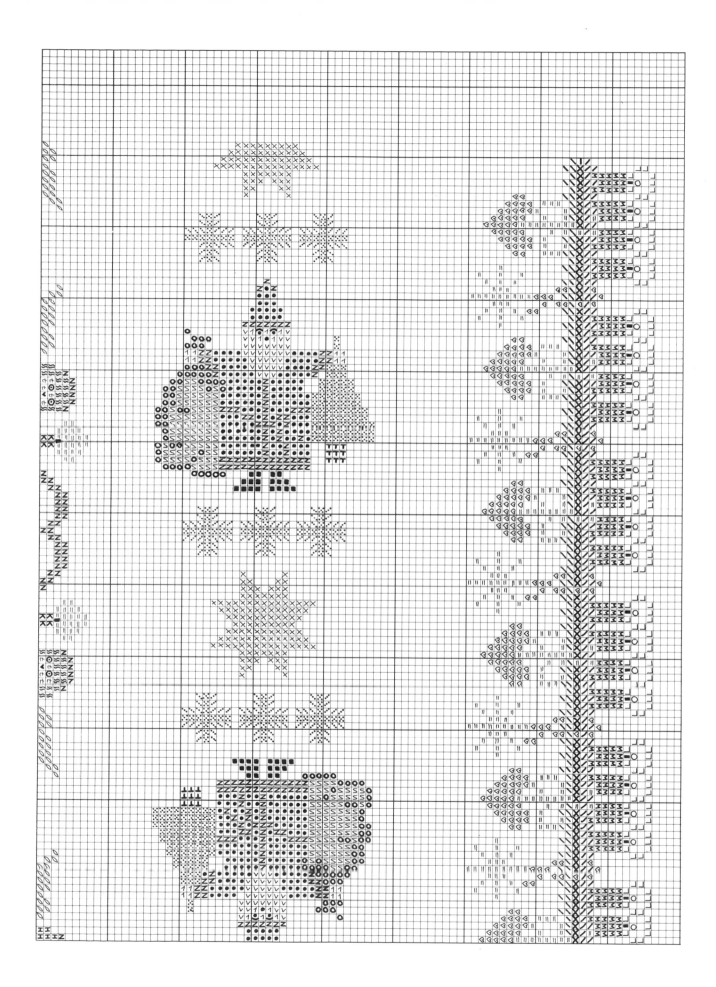

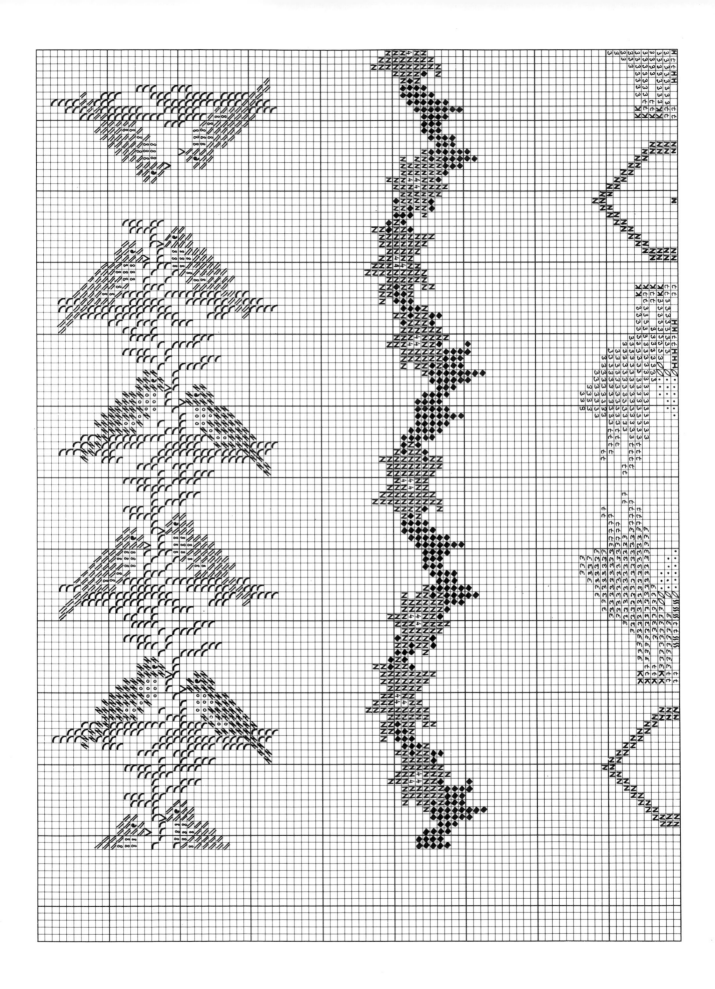

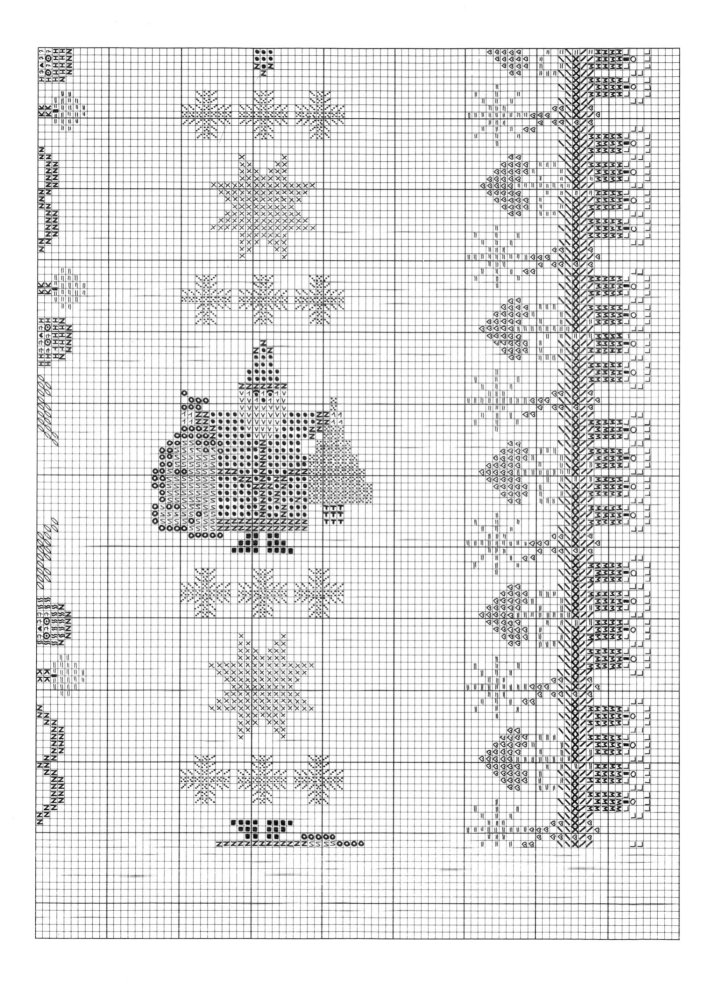

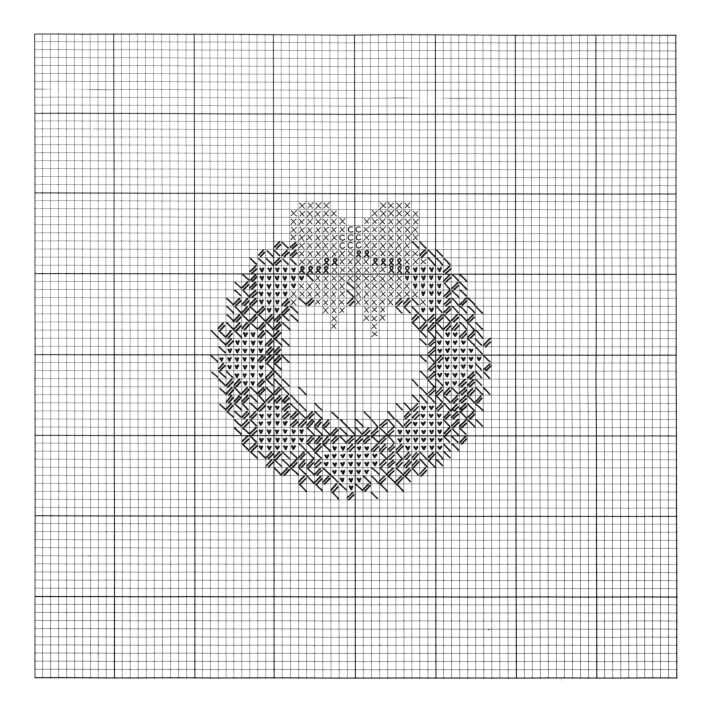

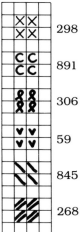

298

891

306

59

845

268

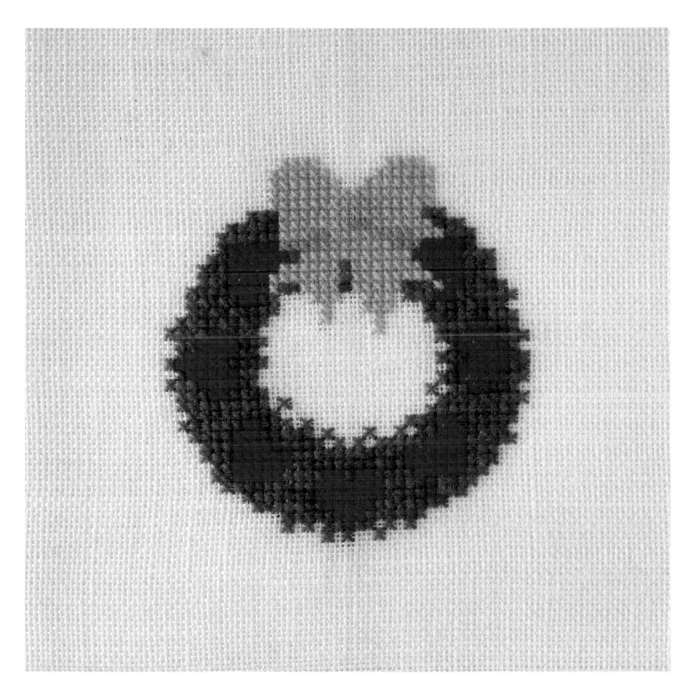

A pretty and easy motif—even for a beginner. It is best to start the project in the center of the bow, which acts as a point of orientation for counting the stitches that follow.

Size: 2⅓ × 2⅓ inches (6 × 6cm)

Time: appr. 5 hours

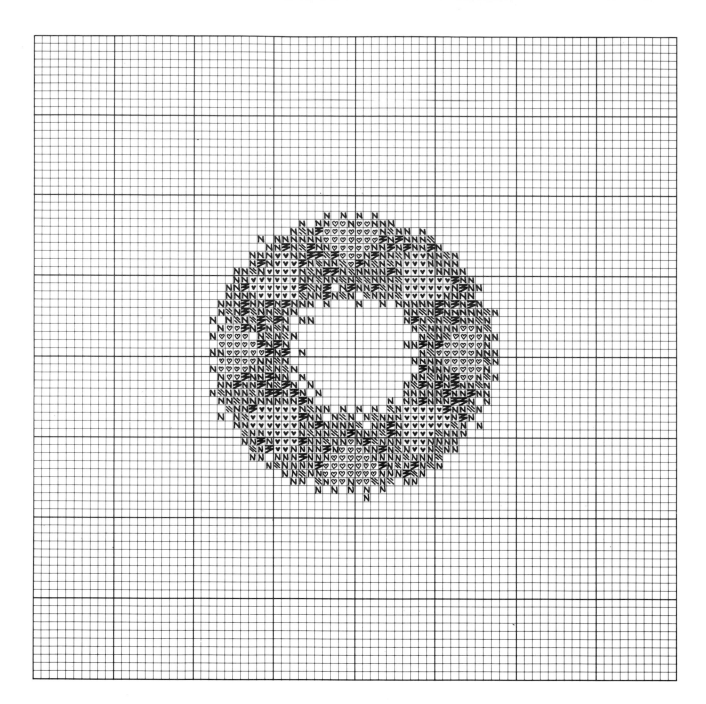

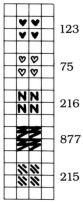

123

75

216

877

215

This wreath can be easily mastered by a beginner. Starting point should be the heart at the top of the wreath.

Size: 2¼ × 2¼ inches (5 × 5 cm)

Time appr. 5 hours

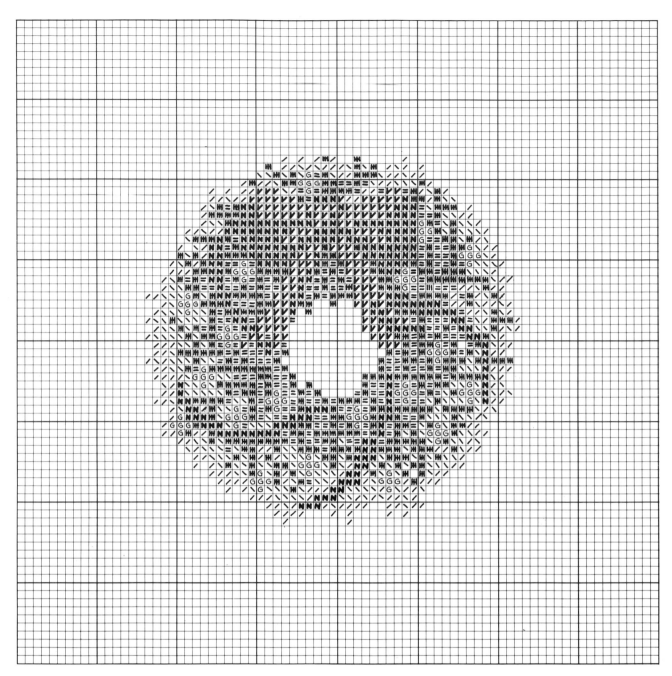

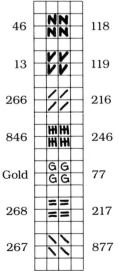

46	**N**	118
13	**V**	119
266	/	216
846	**H**	246
Gold	**G**	77
268	=	217
267	\	877

The sampler shown offers two different color combinations: one in the traditional red/green combination and the other in cool, Nordic colors. This provides examples of what can be achieved with different color schemes. Use your imagination and create your own.

Size: 3⅛ × 3⅛ inches (8 × 8cm)

Time: appr. 7 hours

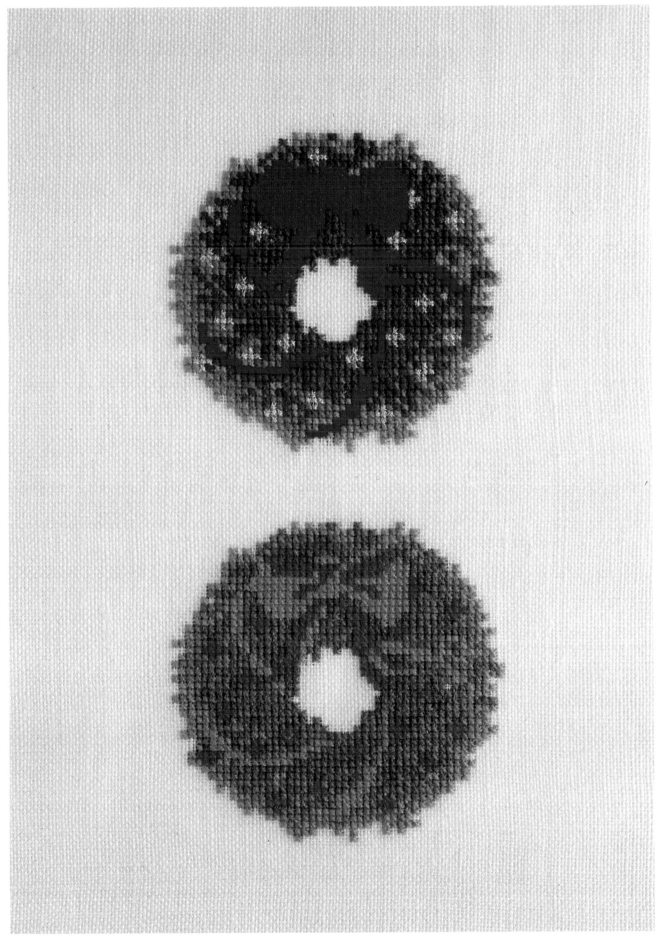

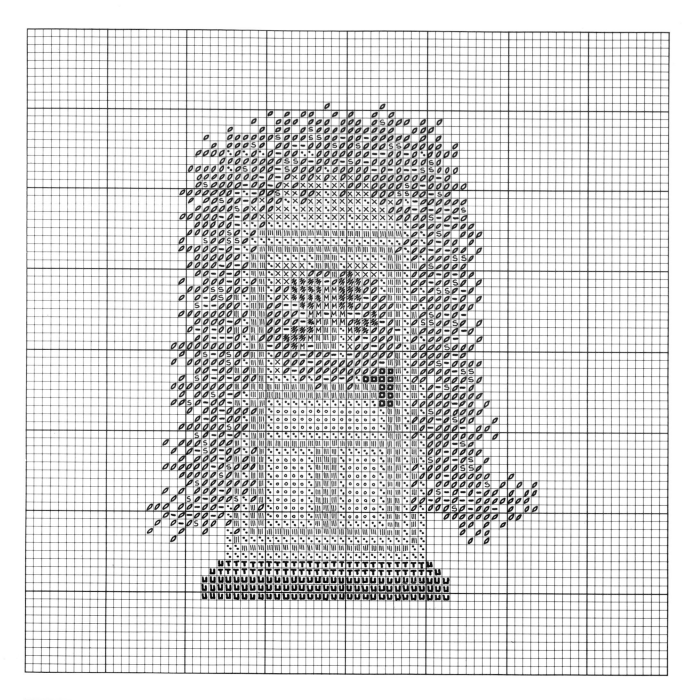

⌀⌀ / ⌀⌀	268	
S S / S S	Silver	
− − / − −	846	
∴ ∴ / ∴ ∴	900	
▣▣ / ▣▣	400	
X X / X X	298	

⦀⦀ / ⦀⦀	146	
o o / o o	847	
U U / U U	393	
T T / T T	392	
⅍⅍ / ⅍⅍	46	
M M / M M	47	

This door, decorated festively for Christmas, indicates the coziness that resides behind it.

Size: 4⅛ × 3⅓ inches (10.5 × 8.5cm)

Time: appr. 15 hours

(#381: halfstitch; S: silver)

●● ●●	355	◥	381 half	X X X X	298	⫽⫽ ⫽⫽	244	•• ••	2
∘ ∘ ∘ ∘	914	σ σ σ σ	279	▬	306	Z Z Z Z	59	W W W W	940
●● ●●	358	T T T T	168	W W	109	⫶• •⫶	928	ℓ ℓ ℓ ℓ	847
■■ ■■	381	‖‖‖ ‖‖‖	54	♡ ♡	75	∥ ∥	118	S S S S	Silver

This cheerful teddy bear, resting in a gift box, is undoubtedly looking forward to Christmas. Several hours should be set aside for this sampler by those who would like to enjoy the finished project.

Size: 5½ × 4⅓ inches (14 × 11cm)

Time: appr. 20 hours

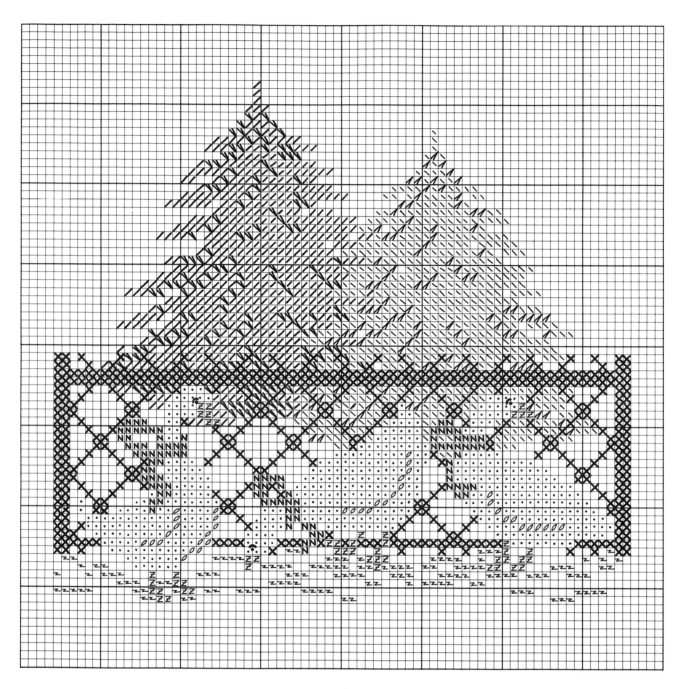

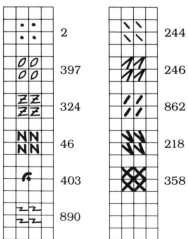

• • / • •	2	
∅ ∅ / ∅ ∅	397	
Ƶ Ƶ / Ƶ Ƶ	324	
N N / N N	46	
໒	403	
⇄ / ⇄	890	

\ \ / \ \	244	
〃 〃 / 〃 〃	246	
/ / / / /	862	
⩔ ⩔	218	
⊠	358	

Instead of ending up in the oven for the Christmas dinner, these wonderfully decorated geese will survive and add to the festive decoration of many a holiday to come.

Size: 4¼ × 4¾ inches (11 × 12.2cm)

Time: 12 hours

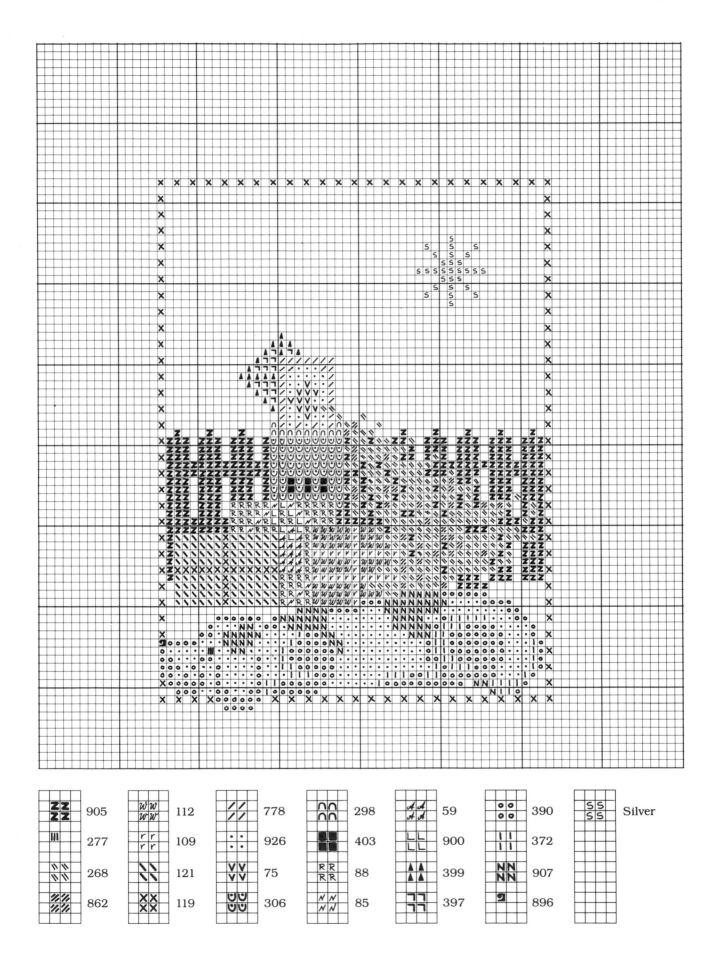

Z Z / **Z Z**	905	w w / w w	112	/ / / /	778	∩ ∩ / ∩ ∩	298	A A / A A	59	o o / o o	390	S S / S S	Silver
‖‖	277	r r / r r	109	· · / · ·	926	■■ / ■■	403	L L / L L	900	I I / I I	372		
∖∖ / ∖∖	268	∖∖ / ∖∖	121	V V / V V	75	R R / R R	88	▲ ▲ / ▲ ▲	399	N N / N N	907		
▨▨ / ▨▨	862	X X / X X	119	∪∪ / ∪∪	306	N N / N N	85	⌐⌐ / ⌐⌐	397	⅃	896		

The gifts that Santa has left at the garden fence are well guarded. Did he leave them there because he was afraid to come down the chimney? Those who love dogs should particularly enjoy this sampler.

Size: 4¼ × 3⅝ inches (11 × 8.5cm)

Time: 13 hours

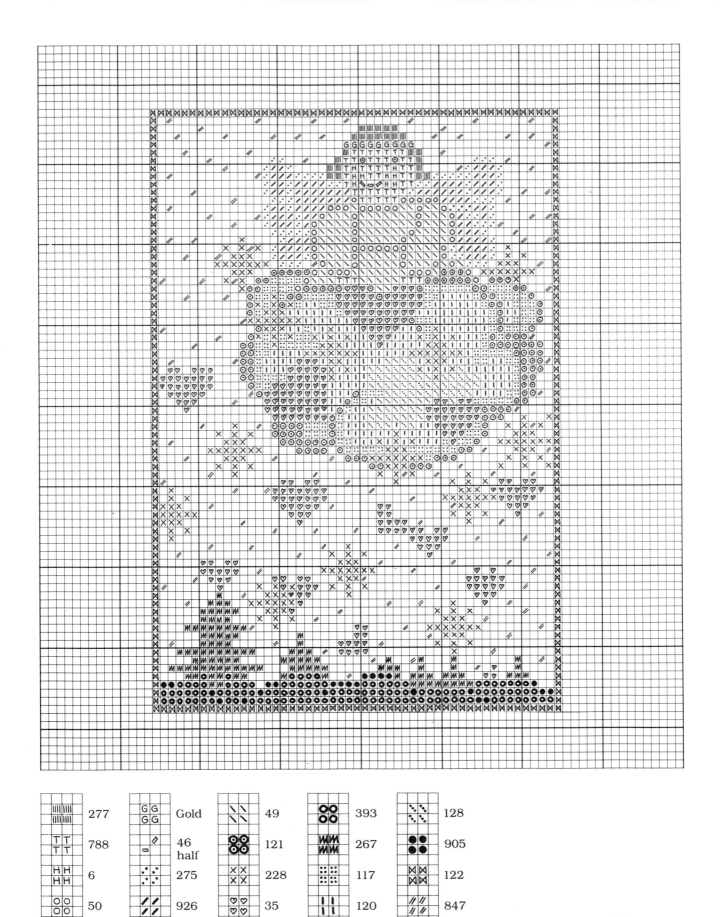

277	Gold	49	393	128
788	46 half	121	267	905
6	275	228	117	122
50	926	35	120	847

This sampler symbolizes Christmas. Perched on a cloud is an angel, hoping that the spirit of the season will reach everybody on Earth. There are stars that bring the message of Christmas, and hearts that represent love and warmth. This project is easy to complete.

Size: 5⅛ × 3½ inches (13 × 8.5cm)

Time: 8 hours

At last we know where Santa buys his clothes! Too bad we can't look beyond the display window.

This is a project for people with patience. The needles on the evergreen branches are half-stitches, either pointing to the left or to the right.

Pattern for this sampler is on pages 40 and 41.

Size: 6 × 8¼ inches (15.5 × 21cm)

Time: 38 hours

(Symbols #397: halfstitch; #905: straight-stitch; #19: straightstitch; #403: wick; G: Gold; #246: straightstitch; S: Silver)

◆◆/◆◆	403 halfstitch	⋀⋀/⋀⋀	358	‖‖/‖‖	339
■■/■■	403	8 8/8 8	279	KK/KK	100
·.·/·:·	9	·:·/·:·	280	▮	403 wick
▲▲	13	↗↗/↗↗	355	GG/GG	Gold
SS/SS	900	h h/h h	907	⫽⫽	246 halfstitch
⫽⫽/⫽⫽	397 halfstitch	ЄЄ/ЄЄ	365	8 8/8 8	47
●●/●●	46	⊢⊢/⊢⊢	123	⫴⫴/⫴⫴	118
⋈⋈/⋈⋈	22	••••	905 straight	SS/SS	Silver
· ·/· ·	847	NN/NN	905	▦	341
ƒƒ/ƒƒ	373	XX/XX	298	ᒋᒋ/ᒋᒋ	233
ZZ/ZZ	922	⋀⋀	375	°°/°°	398
⬡⬡/⬡⬡	850	n n/n n	50	⨃⨃/⨃⨃	862
CC/CC	306	m m/m m	40		
▼▼	112	⦰⦰/⦰⦰	117		
cc/cc	400	⦰⦰/⦰⦰	120		
⋀⋀/⋀⋀	188	==/==	778		
>>/>>	277	⌐	13 straight		
99/99	218	⌢⌢	145		

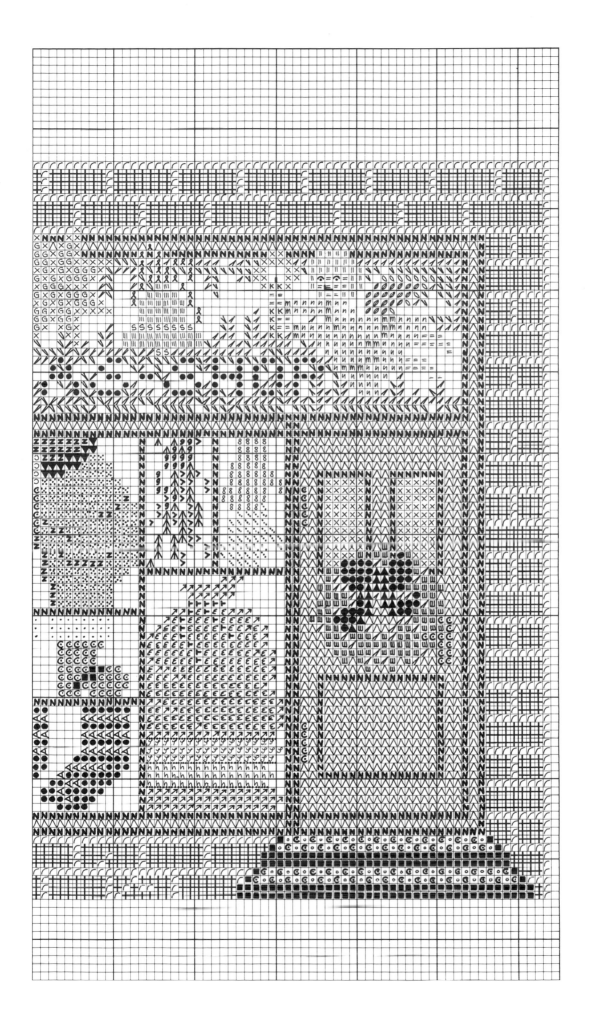

Relaxed and content, Santa Claus is on his way to his next stop, bringing gifts and the spirit of the season. Speaking of spirits, what do you think is in the bottle under his seat?

Size: $2\frac{5}{8} \times 7\frac{2}{3}$ inches (6.6 × 19.5cm)

Time: 13 hours

(Symbols for #59: lips; #403: halfstitch)

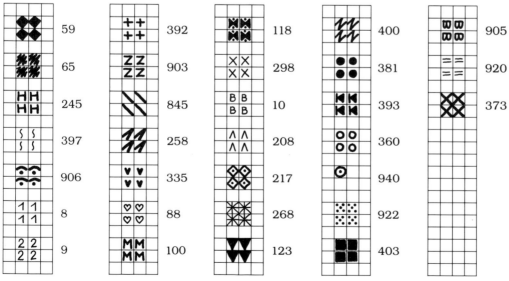

59	392	118
65	903	298
245	845	10
397	258	208
906	335	217
8	88	268
9	100	123

400	905	
381	920	
393	373	
360		
940		
922		
403		

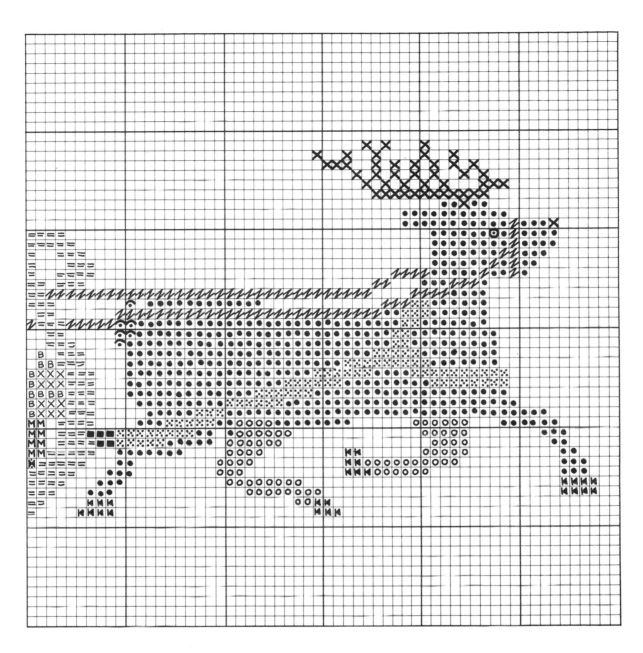

Zählmuster zum Schlitten-Motiv auf den Seiten
44 und 45

⌇⌇	397	❖❖	65	⫽⫽	358	◷◷	400	³³	118	ee	145	RR	970	++	375
11	914	∴∴	390	MM	360	◼◼	403	EE	119	tt	778	vv	279		
⋯⋯	10	⋰⋰	59	BB	121	⦚⦚	890	NN	100	◜	403 half	99	969		
◠◠	920	⫽⫽	217	22	373	≡≡	112	ᴗ	35	◤◤	845	⫽⫽	77		
●●	59	⫽⫽	263	✻✻	905	44	88	∘∘	893	◥◥	846	✖✖	903		

The inspiration for this Santa came from an old Christmas cookie mold.

Be careful when washing, since the dye in the red floss used for Santa's coat might bleed. When steam-ironing, put a protective layer of crepe paper between the finished sampler and the surface of the ironing board so that the excess dye can be absorbed into the protective material. Embroidery is always ironed face down. If a damp cloth is used instead of the steam-ironing method, make sure that it is almost dry.

Size: 7¼ × 6¼ inches (18.5 × 15.5cm)

Time: appr. 18 hours

(Symbol #46: lips)

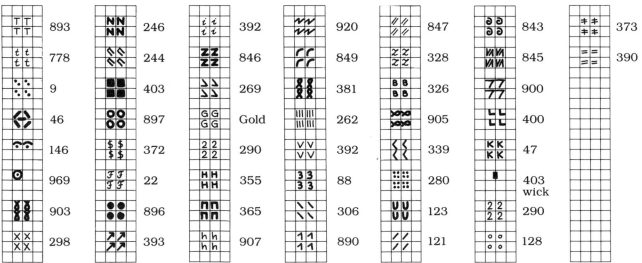

TT / TT	893	
tt / tt	778	
∴∴	9	
◈	46	
⌒⌒	146	
◉	969	
𝄞𝄞	903	
XX / XX	298	

NN / NN	246	
◊◊	244	
■■	403	
OO	897	
$$ / $$	372	
ℱℱ	22	
●●	896	
↗↗	393	

ii / ii	392	
ZZ	846	
↘↘	269	
GG	Gold	
22	290	
HH	355	
⊓⊓	365	
hh	907	

∿∿	920	
⌠⌠	849	
✕✕	381	
‖‖	262	
VV	392	
33	88	
\\	306	
11	890	

// //	847	
ZZ	328	
BB	326	
✕✕	905	
⟨⟨	339	
⁖⁖	280	
UU	123	
//	121	

◔◔	843	
⋁⋁	845	
77	900	
⌐⌐	400	
KK	47	
■	403 wick	
22	290	
oo	128	

≠≠	373	
==	390	

On a crisp, starry night, three children singing Christmas carols bring us the joyous news of Christ's birth. What could be more traditional? Note that the lips of the children are a combination of vertical and horizontal, straight half-stitches. The eyes can be done in either cross-stitch or in small knot-stitches.

Size: 7 × 6 inches (17.5 × 15cm)

Time: 18 hours

(Symbol #683: halfstitch; #246: halfstitch)

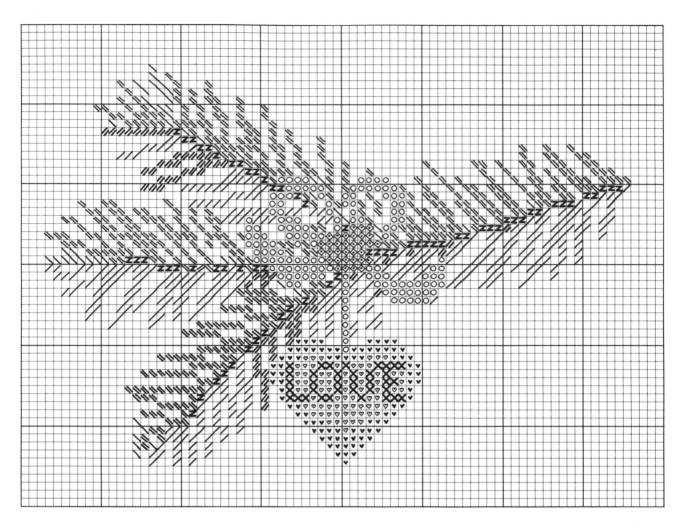

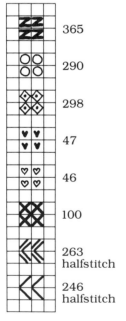

ZZ ZZ	365
OO OO	290
⬧⬧ ⬧⬧	298
♥♥ ♥♥	47
♡♡ ♡♡	46
✖✖	100
⫽⫽	263 halfstitch
⟍⟋	246 halfstitch

This sampler requires close attention. It is easy to lose count when working the halfstitches of the evergreen branches. It is best to start in the center with the yellow bow, then do the heart, and work from there to the outside.

Size: 4×5⅛ inches (10×13cm)

Time: 6 hours

Above: The sampler for the pattern on the opposite page.

Below: Symbols for the sampler on page 52.

m m / m m	146	R R / R R	88	Ø Ø / Ø Ø	65	123	X X / X X	290	= =	232	≀ ≀	244	∙ ∙ / ∙ ∙	847
v v / v v	398	U U / U U	112	∙∙∙∙	35	218	+ + / + +	306	/ / / /	778	ss / ss	358	4 4 / 4 4	326
L L / L L	905	862	S S / S S	Silver	Λ Λ / Λ Λ	59	M M / M M	890	r r / r r	920	7 7 / 7 7	188	a a / a a	313
N N / N N	846	● ● / ● ●	46	G G / G G	Gold	= = / = =	400	I I / I I	393	\ \ / \ \	128	⋈ ⋈ / ⋈ ⋈	118	W W / W W	860
267	o o / o o	98	ℛ ℛ / ℛ ℛ	121	▮	403 wick	∴ ∙ / ∙∴	401	⁰ ⁰ / ⁰ ⁰	49	⌐ ⌐ / ⌐ ⌐	109		

Symbols for this pattern are on page 51.

Santa was here!

The lips of each of the angels are done in one straight, vertical stitch, and one halfstitch. The eyes are small knot-stitches. The wreath on the door is made with one vertical stitch each in sil-verfloss between two green cross-stitches. While the door panel is made with full cross-stitches, the frames around them are halfstitches, running alternately in opposite directions.

Time appr. 20 hours

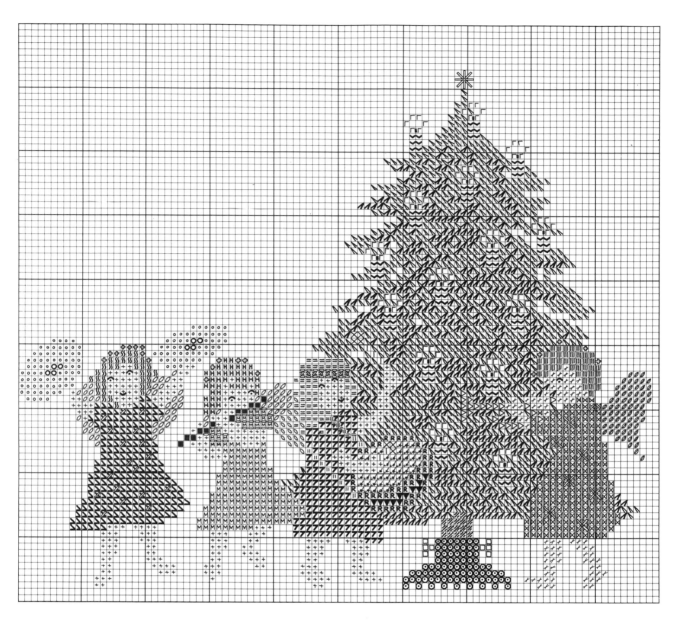

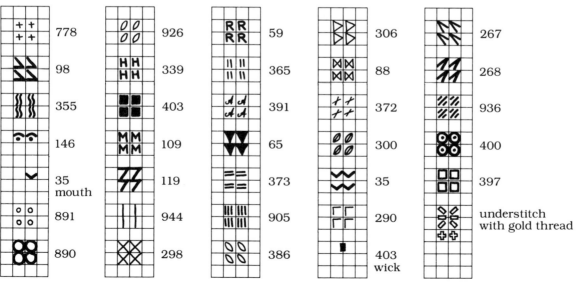

++ / ++	778	
(98 symbol)	98	
(355 symbol)	355	
(146 eyes)	146	
(mouth symbol)	35 mouth	
o o / o o	891	
(890 symbol)	890	

00 / 00	926	
HH / HH	339	
■■ / ■■	403	
MM / MM	109	
(119 symbol)	119	
				944	
XX	298	

RR / RR	59	
							365	
AA / AA	391	
▼▼	65	
== / ==	373	
							905	
00 / 00	386	

▷◁	306	
⋈⋈	88	
++ / ++	372	
00 / 00	300	
⌄⌄	35	
ΓΓ / ΓΓ	290	
▮	403 wick	

(267 symbol)	267	
(268 symbol)	268	
// / //	936	
⊙⊙	400	
□□ / □□	397	
(understitch symbol)	understitch with gold thread	

54

The inspiration for this sampler came from a Christmas carol of the year 1623, which speaks of angels singing, playing the recorder, the drums, and the cymbals: all rejoicing in the spirit of the season.

Size: 5½ × 6¾ inches (13.5 × 17cm)

Time: appr. 13 hours

This sampler extends wishes for a Merry Christmas in ten languages. (Color design: Angela Kerzel.) Of course each individual motif can be used separately in combination with the language appropriate to the person for whom it is intended. Choice of colors can be changed also. This might be an ideal project for using leftover floss. Pattern for the sampler is on pages 58 and 59.

Size: 12 × 9¼ inches (30 × 23.5cm)
Time: 50 hours

Symbol	Color	Symbol	Color	Symbol	Color	Symbol	Color	Symbol	Color
XX	118	MM	360	V	9	♡♡	65	33	379
88	95	oo	336	(half)	54 half	⋀⋀	301	エエ	22
IIIII	75	●●	13	IIII	54	VV	133	⊔⊔	275
KK	119	BB	146	GG	Gold	DD	845	II	400
▮	403 wick	rr	85	◥◤	145	dd	281	SSSS	900
XX	105	⅃	358	XX	105	MM	890	NN	897
⌐⌐	267	bb	375	HH	928	NN	891	σσ	88
SS	Silver	VV	373	∴∴	313	IIII	306	↗↗	269
NN	261	++	244	■■	403	ff	8	⋙⋙	268 border
11	860	#	877	⋀⋀	326	~~	117	aa	159
MM	77	ℓℓ	109	ZZ	324	♡♭	65 half	OO	300
♡♡	65	⋅⋅	292	°°°°	10	⋀⋀	100	77	365
∴∴	280	ꟿꟿ	217	ℓℓ	338	∞∞	98	♡	65 knot
⊐⊐	843	SS	Silver	ΓΓ	216	ii	96	♥	133 knot
EE	355	hh	206	⟨⟨⟨	267	✳	400	11	128
88	969	∏∏	6	⌇⌇	261	88	168		

FROHE WEIHNACHTEN
MERRY CHRISTMAS
JOYEUX NOEL   GOD JUL
BOAS FESTAS   FELIZ NAVIDAD
HYVÄÄ JOULUA
PRETTIGE KERSTDAGEN
BUON NATALE   FELICES PASCUASY

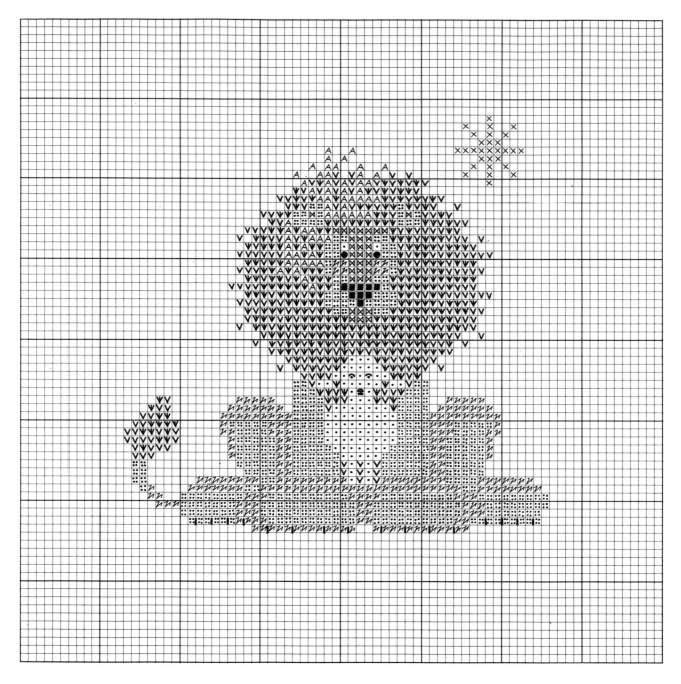

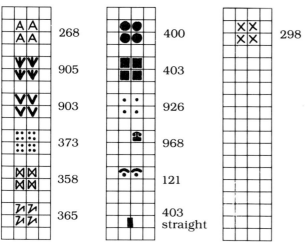

A A / A A — 268	● ● / ● ● — 400	X X / X X — 298
▼▼ / ▼▼ — 905	■ ■ / ■ ■ — 403	
▼V / ▼V — 903	∴ ∴ / ∴ ∴ — 926	
∴∴ / ∴∴ — 373	☎ — 968	
⋈⋈ / ⋈⋈ — 358	◠◠ — 121	
𝄞𝄞 / 𝄞𝄞 — 365	▮ — 403 straight	

The symbol of the lion and the lamb: a sampler that expresses our hope for peace. (Design: Katja Mackens Hassler.)

Size: 3¾ × 3¾ inches (9.5 × 9.5cm)

Time: appr. 6 hours

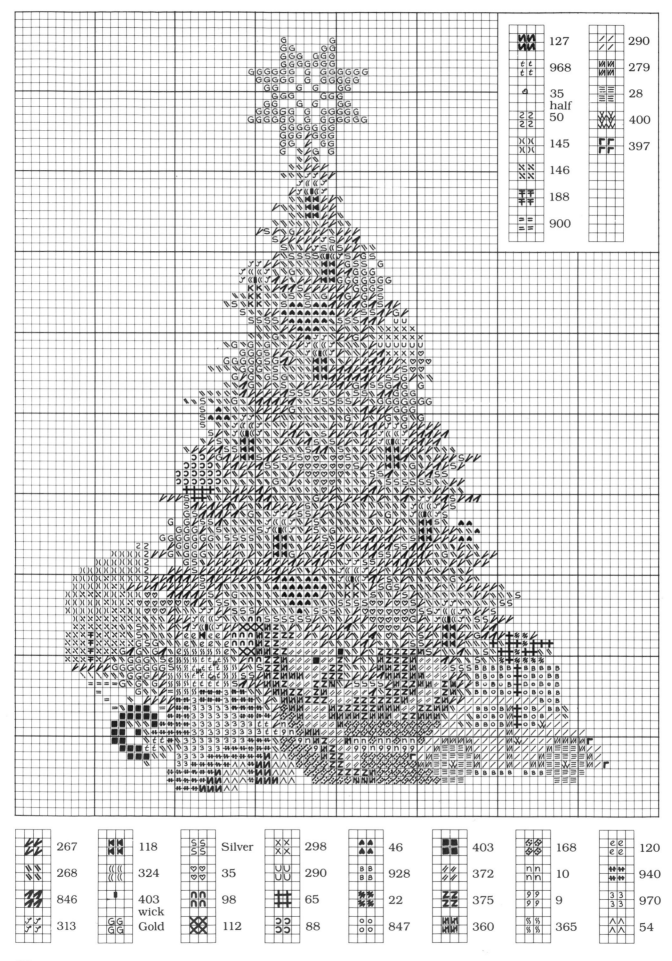

Memories of Christmas past are awakened with this Christmas tree decorated in full splendor. And everybody will find a present among the many left under the tree!

Size: 6⅜ × 4½ inches (16 × 11.5cm)

Time: 15 hours

INDEX